M Y S T E R I E S

OF THE ANCIENT WORLD

LOST ATLANTIS

JENNIFER WESTWOOD

WEIDENFELD & NICOLSON

LONDON

A great imperial power destroyed by a cataclysm, an island sunk beneath the sea: this is the tragedy of Atlantis. Is the story true, and if so where *was* the lost island? Classical scholars, mythologists, archaeologists, historians, anthropologists,

geophysicists, science-fiction writers, occultists (and others) have all had their ideas, coloured by their own preoccupations. So far, no location suggested has stood the test of time, each generation dismantling the arguments of the last in search of its own answers.

The story

Let us begin at the beginning, with two 'dialogues' composed by the Greek philosopher Plato a little more than 2,300 years ago. They are imaginary conversations between Socrates (before 469–399 bc) and three friends, and they are called after their main speakers *Timaeus* and *Critias*.

In them, Critias, Plato's maternal great-grandfather, tells a story he heard as a child from *his* grandfather, Critias the Elder (d. 403 BC), then a man of nearly 90. The elder Critias himself heard it from his father, Dropides, who heard it from his friend, the great Athenian law-giver Solon (*c*.640–*c*.559 BC). Solon said he was told it by an aged priest at the temple of Sais, Egypt, where it was preserved in ancient records.

*T*he island of Atlantis (opposite), outside the Pillars of Heracles. From Athanasius Kircher's **Mundus Subterraneus (1678).**

*P*lato (c.427–347 BC), the Greek philosopher whose account of Atlantis is the only independent source for the story (Paris, Louvre).

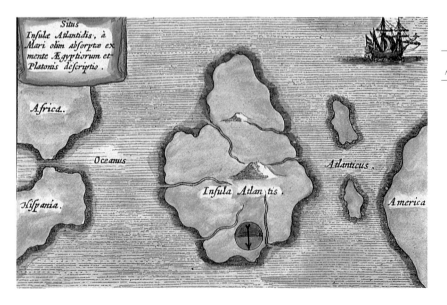

This story, apparently handed down in Plato's own family, is the tale of how
ancient Athens had checked a mighty power which 9,000 years before had
launched an attack on the cities of Europe and Asia from its base in the
Atlantic:

> *There was an island opposite the strait which you call . . . the Pillars of Heracles,*
> *an island larger than Libya and Asia combined . . . On this island of Atlantis had*
> *arisen a powerful and remarkable dynasty of kings, who. . . controlled, within the*
> *strait, Libya up to Egypt and Europe as far as Tyrrhenia [Italy]. This dynasty . . .*
> *attempted to enslave at a single stroke . . . all the territory within the straight.*

Athens led an alliance of the Greeks against the invaders, and when they
deserted her fought on alone. Victorious, the Athenians liberated those who
had fallen under the Atlantean yoke.

> *At a later time there were earthquakes and floods of extraordinary violence, and in a*
> *single dreadful day and night . . . the island of Atlantis . . . was swallowed up by the*
> *sea and vanished; this is why the sea in that area is to this day impassable to navigation,*
> *which is hindered by mud just below the surface, the remains of the sunken island . . .*

5

In the *Critias*, after describing ancient Athens, Critias recounts the origins of the Atlanteans, descendants of Poseidon, god of the sea and earthquakes, and gives an account of their mountainous but fertile island, rich in timber, minerals and animals, including 'numerous elephants'.

He describes their extraordinary capital city, built around an acropolis, on which stood their palace, in the middle of which, surrounded by a golden wall, was Poseidon's temple, huge and 'somewhat outlandish'. Hot and cold springs fed open pools and covered hot baths for winter use, with separate arrangements for kings, commoners, women, horses and other beasts of burden.

The acropolis was defended by five concentric rings of alternating water and land, connected by bridges and tunnels. The two land rings held temples and gardens, exercise grounds and a racecourse. The three water rings, linked to the sea by a wide canal, enabled ships to sail into the heart of the city.

The ten kings of Atlantis were descendants of five pairs of twins, all sons, born by the mortal Cleito to Poseidon. They ruled under the suzerainty of the house of Atlas, the eldest, from whom Atlantis took its name. Every fifth or

*T*he so-called Cross of Atlantis, a symbolic representation of the acropolis ringed by land and water described by Plato.

*P*oseidon (right), god of the sea and earthquakes, ancestor of the Atlantean kings (bronze, c.460–450 BC, Athens, National Archaeological Museum).

sixth year they assembled for consultation in Poseidon's temple; before deliberations began, the kings, armed with clubs and nooses, hunted the sacred bulls roaming at large there, and sacrificed one to Poseidon.

After many generations the Atlanteans degenerated from a noble super-race into greedy aggressors. Almighty Zeus decided to punish them and called an assembly of the gods. At this point Critias's narrative breaks off. The dialogue was left unfinished.

*P*lato – called the
first science-
fiction writer –
intentionally made his
Atlantis alien and
exotic. From Sir Gerald
Hargreave's **Atlantis**
(1954).

Atlantis-in-the-Atlantic

Argument over whether Plato's lost paradise was ever a real place began within
50 years of his death in 348/7 bc. His pupil Aristotle thought it was a political
fable. By the time Pliny the Elder came to write his *Natural History* (ad 77) opinion was divided into two camps: believers and sceptics.

But, if a fact, where was it? Accepting Plato's description of it as lying opposite the 'Pillars of Heracles', which in the ancient world normally meant the

Straits of Gibraltar, it was in the Atlantic. From the first this lent the story great mystique. The ancient Greeks envisaged the Atlantic as part of the ocean which encircled the world, and though the adventurous Carthaginians had sailed through the Pillars of Heracles, and up and down the coast, the Greeks knew little of it, believing it unnavigable.

To the Roman historian Tacitus, writing in ad 98, the Atlantic was still the 'unknown sea'. This reputation is precisely why many other mysterious,

paradisal islands were located in it – the Fortunate Isles, the Island of the Seven Cities, Maida, St Brendan's Isle, Hy Breasil. They were long marked on maps and sought on voyages of discovery – Hy Breasil was only dropped from mariners' charts in 1865.

Meantime, in 1553, about 50 years after Columbus discovered America, the Spanish historian

I llustration of 1499 of the **Voyage of Brendan** *(11th century). St Brendan's Isle, the mythical object of his voyage, was last searched for in the 18th century.*

R ock of Gibraltar, one of the Pillars *of Heracles. Beyond lay ancient Tartessos, near Cadiz, mooted as an Atlantean colony.*

11

Francesco López de Gómara pointed out that the West Indies and the American continent pretty well matched Plato's account of a 'continent' lying beyond Atlantis. Thereafter, that Atlantis was in the New World found many advocates, not least Francis Bacon in his utopian *Nova Atlantis* (1614–18).

The idea of America as Atlantis faded as more was learned of the New World, but Atlantis continued to be placed in the Atlantic. Athanasius Kircher, in *Mundus Subterraneus* (1655), suggested that the Azores were the mountain peaks of the sunken land; others pointed to the Madeiras and Canaries.

The most influential advocate of Atlantis-in-the-Atlantic was the American writer Ignatius Donnelly (1831–1901), who in 1882 published *Atlantis: The Antediluvian World*. Plato's Atlantis, 'larger than Asia and Libya' (Asia Minor and North Africa) amounts to a sizable landmass. Following Kircher, Donnelly proposed that this drowned 'continent' was represented by the Azores, the volcanic tops of a structure called the Mid-Atlantic Ridge, discovered in the 1870s, that runs roughly north to south down the centre of the Atlantic Basin.

At the time, Donnelly's ideas

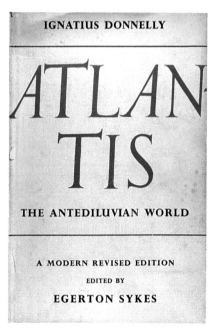

IGNATIUS DONNELLY

ATLAN TIS

THE ANTEDILUVIAN WORLD

A MODERN REVISED EDITION

EDITED BY

EGERTON SYKES

A tlantis: The Antediluvian World *(1882) by Ignatius Donnelly, which popularized the idea of a lost continent in the Atlantic.*

M ayan vase, Tikal, Guatemala. *The anthropologist Lewis Spence (1874–1955) thought the Mayans belong to an Atlantean 'culture-complex' embracing Central America, North Africa and Spain.*

seemed to have at least some scientific basis, but his case was destroyed by discoveries made in the 1960s supporting the theory of 'plate tectonics'. Briefly, most earth scientists now accept that the crust forming the Atlantic ocean floor was never continent-building material; and that the volcanic peaks along the Mid-Atlantic Ridge, rather than being relics of a sunken continent, are comparatively young. As far as science is concerned, the spectre of a submerged continent in the Atlantic has been laid to rest.

*T*he 'Lady of Elche'
(5th century BC), found
at Elche, near Alicante, Spain, once
hailed as an Atlantean priestess
(Madrid, Archaeological Museum).

15

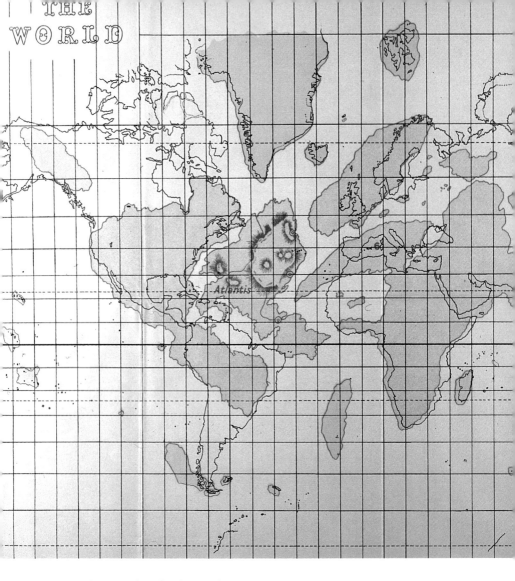

Occult Atlantis

This may not be quite the end of it, though. The Atlantic was also a favourite location for psychics and occultists drawn to Atlantean studies in the 19th and 20th centuries. Using clairvoyance, psychic intuition, hypnotic regression to former lives and the 'Akashic Records', a history of all past events said by

Rudolf Steiner (1861–1925) to exist on the astral plane, occultists claimed that Atlantis existed in an almost unbelievably ancient past – long before scientists place the first appearance of man on the planet – and that it was the source of a secret wisdom.

*M**ap from* **The Story** *of* **Atlantis** *(1896) by W. Scott-Elliott, pioneer of occult studies of Atlantis.*

*T**oltec warrior, Tula, Mexico. Scott-Elliott says Atlantis was ruled by Toltecs, who enslaved its 3 m tall black aboriginals.*

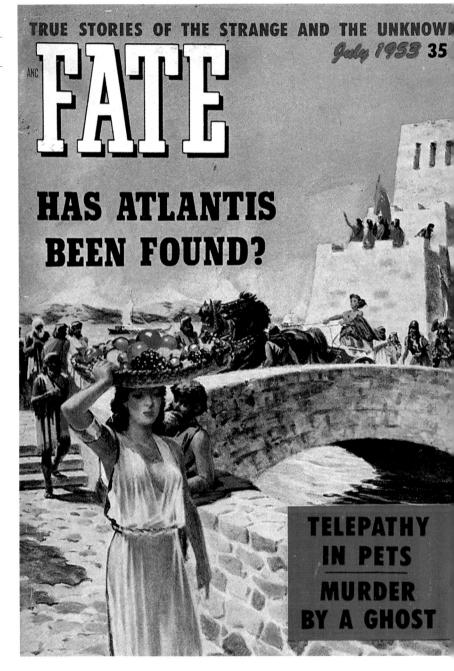

TRUE STORIES OF THE STRANGE AND THE UNKNOWN

July 1953 35

ANC

FATE

HAS ATLANTIS BEEN FOUND?

TELEPATHY IN PETS

MURDER BY A GHOST

This brings us to Atlantology – as Atlantis-hunting has come to be known. The term is often used to imply a certain dottiness by sober scholars perturbed at the claims made by some Atlantologists in defence of their theories, as when Frank Joseph in *Atlantis in Wisconsin* (1995) argues that the reason other divers have not seen the structures he reports is because they shift into another dimension. A degree of obsessiveness attaches to the subject and fraud is not unknown: Paul Schliemann, grandson of Heinrich Schliemann, the discoverer of Troy, in 1912 claimed to have learned from his grandfather of a bowl he found at Troy, inscribed 'From King Chronos of Atlantis'. This bowl proved to be a fake when examined.

Wishful thinking is exceedingly common. Excitement was great in the late 1960s over the so-called 'Bimini Road', a J-shaped configuration of stones lying about 6 m underwater off the coast of North Bimini, Bahamas, sighted in 1968 and hailed as an ancient man-made pavement. Along with a building alleged to be a pre-Columbian temple, found a year earlier off Andros, it was said to confirm predictions made by the American medium Edgar Cayce (1877–1945), concerning the reappearance of Atlantis: 'expect it in '68 or'69.' As it turned out, the 'temple' was a sponge store built in the 1930s, and in 1981 the US Geological Survey produced conclusive evidence that the 'Bimini' Road was laid down by natural means a mere 2,500–3,500 years ago.

C over of **Fate magazine,** *July 1953.*

Diving for Atlantis around the Atlantic will doubtless continue in the teeth of the evidence, because what fuels the quest is romance. For centuries, legends of 'sunken cities' have existed along the Atlantic coast, many of them based on occasional glimpses by fishermen and other seafarers of what look like sunken 'roads' and 'walls'. In addition, great discoveries in underwater archaeology, such as the remains of the Pharos Lighthouse, one of the Seven Wonders of the World, in Alexandria harbour in the mid-1990s, lures amateur archaeologists on.

*T*he bull,
sacred to
Poseidon, was a
cult animal in
Atlantis, as in
ancient Crete.
Bull's head rhyton,
from Knossos
(Heraklion
Museum).

*T*he royal bull
hunt of
Atlantis has echoes
of the ceremonial
bull game depicted
in a Minoan fresco
at Knossos.

The Mediterranean Solution

Many Atlantis-seekers have ignored Plato's statement that the Atlantean power was based in the Atlantic. The 17th-century Swedish scholar Olaüs Rudbeck located Atlantis in Sweden. In 1762 Frederick Baër equated the ten Atlantean kingdoms with the *twelve* tribes of Israel and the Atlantic with the Red Sea. The 18th-century French astronomer Jean Bailly placed the lost island off Spitsbergen. By the late 19th century, it had also been discovered in the

Sahara, the Caucasus, South Africa, Ceylon, Brazil, Greenland, the British Isles, Prussia and the Netherlands. Rand and Rose Flem-Ath in *When the Sky Fell* (1995) make a case for Antarctica.

The ancient Greeks applied the name 'Pillars of Heracles' not only to the

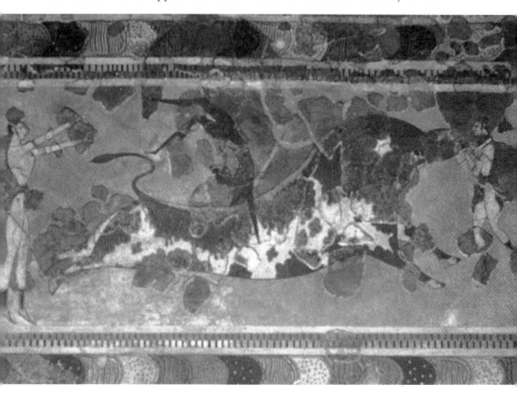

Straits of Gibraltar, but also to the narrow Straits of the Dardanelles, the entrance to the Black Sea. This has encouraged searchers for Atlantis to look within the Mediterranean world.

In 1900, the archaeologist Sir Arthur Evans discovered the Palace of Knossos on Crete, and dubbed the prehistoric civilization he found there 'Minoan'. In February 1909 an anonymous article appeared in *The Times* under the heading 'The Lost Continent', which suggested that in Minoan Crete Evans had

*B*as-relief from
Knossos, Crete.
Was this bull adorning
a Minoan palace the
model for those sacred
to the Atlanteans?

also found Atlantis. Later the writer K. T. Frost argued his case more fully. He proposed that the story of Atlantis was an Egyptian memory of Bronze Age Crete, which in the first half of the second millenium bc had dominated the Aegean. He pointed to parallels between Plato's account and Minoan culture, not least that between the Atlantean kings' bull-hunt, and the bull-cult of Crete evidenced by the Greek legend of Theseus and the Minotaur, and by discoveries at Knossos. Unlike Atlantis, Crete had not sunk under the sea, so instead

T he island of Santorini.   Frost suggested that the legend of Theseus preserved the memory of a Mycenaean invasion in about 1450 or 1400 bc that overthrew Cretan civilization.

Frost's theory was remembered by the Greek archaeologist Spyridon Marinatos, when, during excavations in the 1930s on the northern coast of Crete, he found both Minoan remains and quantities of pumice. Only 96 km off was the arc-shaped volcanic island of Thera (modern Santorini), and Marinatos

*S*antorini,
  destroyed
by earthquakes,
was covered
with volcanic
ashes.

26

knew its volcano had erupted in the Bronze Age. In 1939, he proposed that the collapse of Cretan power in the 15th century bc, indicated by the destruction of Knossos and other Minoan cities, was the result of a massive eruption of Thera, resulting in ash-falls and gigantic tidal waves. Returning to Frost's idea of a Minoan Atlantis he began in 1967 to excavate a site near Akrotiri in the south of Thera. He found a great prehistoric city with streets of houses, some still three storeys high, with rooms painted with exquisite frescoes. There were remains of furniture and fine pottery in a style which seemed to show that the

city was both contemporary and probably linked with the Minoan palaces of Crete.

Marinatos and others painted a compelling picture of a prosperous commercial centre of the Minoan civilization which in about 1520 bc was overtaken by disaster. The Theran volcano erupted three times, the third time with a such crack that it may have been heard 3,000 km away (estimates make the eruption four times as powerful as that of Krakatoa in 1883, which was heard in Australia). The volcano blanketed the island with ash, in some places 30 m thick, burying the main city completely. About 40 years later, the volcano's cone collapsed, creating tidal waves which destroyed Cretan civilization.

This dramatic scenario provided both an explanation of the fate of Crete and an original for Atlantis. The Crete-Thera solution became widely accepted, but 20 years on is losing support, not the least difficulty being that Theran ash discovered at other sites on Crete and in the Aegean seems to prove that Thera was destroyed by a single eruption anything up to 150 years earlier than the destruction of the Cretan palaces.

he excavations at Akrotiri. Much of the ancient city still stands.

Shifting the setting closer to the Dardanelles, the geo-archaeologist Bernhard Zangger has since argued in *The Flood from Heaven* (1993) that the tale of Atlantis is an Egyptian version of the Trojan War. Peter James in *The Sunken Kingdom* (1995) similarly looks to modern Turkey for the solution, suggesting

that Atlantis is an echo of what Pliny called 'the very celebrated city . . . that used to be called Tantalis'. According to Pliny it was destroyed by an earthquake and in his time lay under the 'marsh of Sale'. Pausanias (2nd century ad), author of the first guide to Greece, tells a local tale of what seems to be the same city, on Mount Sipylus (modern Manisa Dagi): 'it disappeared into a chasm, and from the fissure in the mountain water gushed forth, and the chasm became named Lake Saloe. The ruins of the city could still be seen in the lake until the water of the torrent covered them up'.

Fact or Fiction?

Plato is the only independent source for the story of Atlantis: everyone else who mentions it derives it from him. For all the theories and excavations, we are no nearer knowing for certain whether or not he made it up.

Some argue that Solon really *did* bring the story back from Egypt. There is nothing inherently impossible in the long chain of oral transmission from Solon to the younger Critias. Advocates of an Egyptian origin point to the similarity of the tale to one known in Egypt during the Middle Kingdom (2000–1750 bc). This is 'The Shipwrecked Traveller', which tells of a man who, after being shipwrecked, was cast up on a paradisal island, where he met a golden dragon. The dragon foretells that the

Volcanic ash thrown into the sky during the eruption of a volcano.

A crater in the volcanic Aeolian Islands, off the coast of Italy.

33

Egyptian will be rescued, but 'never more shall you see this island because it will be swallowed by the waves'.

But if the story of Atlantis was remembered at Sais, as Plato says, why didn't the priests there also tell it to the historian Herodotus (c.454–20 bc), who like Solon visited and talked with them. And would a story that came in its entirety from Egypt contain so much accurate knowledge of prehistoric Athens? For Plato's account is as much about Athens as about Atlantis. He describes a circuit wall on top of the Acropolis, warriors' houses on its northern side, a spring on its top subsequently choked by earthquakes – Mycenaean features all confirmed by archaeology.

These are just a handful of the questions raised by Plato's text. Classical scholars on the whole share Aristotle's view that the story is a moral fable, a composite of ideas, historical facts, and ancient myths of the Golden Age and the Universal Deluge, made by Plato, who wished to explore further the ideal state he had outlined in *The Republic*. They point out that the Atlantis story mirrors the history of the Peloponnesian War (431–404 bc), waged by an Athens that, in the opinion of many of Plato's contemporaries, had no sooner overthrown the Persian Empire than it started empire-building of its own. By a reversal of roles, Atlantis represents the Athens of Plato's time, fallen from greatness; whilst the Athens of his tale is a combination of Sparta, the Athens of Mycenaean days, and the ideal society proposed in *The Republic*. A tantalizing footnote to this reading of the story – remembering that in Plato's account the Athenian army was destroyed during the cataclysm that

*S*olon (c. 640–559 BC), Athenian law-
giver who, according to Plato, brought
the story of Atlantis back from Egypt.
Justus van Ghent, c. 1476.

35

A *thens: the*
Acropolis.
Plato's description
of how it looked in
prehistoric times
is, according to
archaeologists,
highly accurate.

overwhelmed Atlantis – is that in 426 bc, during the Peloponnesian War, a tidal wave wrecked an Athenian fortress on a little island off Locris, in central Greece. Its name was Atalante.

Even if Plato wove the story of Atlantis from an assortment of materials, this is not to say that the whole thing is fiction. And many, perhaps most, people *want* Atlantis to be true. We want our shrinking planet still to contain wonders. We want the promise of great adventures. It is a dull dog indeed who does not thrill to Verne's account in *Twenty Thousand Leagues Under the Sea* (1869) of Arronax's walk with Captain Nemo on the sea-bottom:

> *There were vast heaps of stone . . . There . . . under my eyes, ruined, destroyed, lay a town – its roofs open to the sky . . . Further on, some remains of a giant aqueduct . . . there traces of a quay . . . Further on again, long lines of sunken walls and broad, deserted streets . . . Where was I? where was I? . . . Captain Nemo . . . picking up a piece of chalk . . . advanced to a rock . . . and traced the one word:*
>
> > *A T L A N T I S .*

*I*llustration from an 1870 edition of Jules Verne's **Twenty Thousand Leagues under the Sea.**

LOST
ATLANTIS

PHOTOGRAPHIC ACKNOWLEDGEMENTS
Cover Zefa; pages 2–3 Zefa; p. 4 Peter Clayton
[PC], p. 5 AKG London; p. 6 Mary Evans Picture
Library [MEPL]; p. 7 PC; pp. 8–9 MEPL;
pp. 10–11 Zefa; pp. 11, 12, e.t. archive [ETA];
p. 13 Fortean Picture Library [FPL];
pp. 14–15 ETA; pp. 16–17 MEPL; p. 17 ETA;
p. 18 FPL/Llewellyn Publications; p. 20 PC;
p. 21 ETA; pp. 22–3 AKG; pp. 24–5 Zefa;
pp. 26–7, 28–9 PC; pp. 30–31, 32–3 Zefa;
pp. 34, 36–7 AKG; pp. 38–9 MEPL.

First published in Great Britain 1997
by George Weidenfeld and Nicolson Ltd
The Orion Publishing Group
5 Upper St Martin's Lane
London WC2H 9EA

A CIP catalogue record for this book is available
from the British Library
ISBN 0 297 823051

Picture Research: Suzanne Williams

Design: Harry Green

Typeset in Baskerville